Poems
—FROM THE—
Tree of Life

Rufus Johnson

Poems From the Tree of Life
Copyright © 2026 by Rufus Johnson

ISBN: 979-8999023056 (hc)
ISBN: 979-8999023032 (sc)
ISBN: 979-8999023049 (e)

The Library of Congress Control Number: 2026907067

The views expressed in this book are solely those of the author and reflect the author's own perspectives and experiences.

Rufus Johnson

jrufus52@gmail.com
(804)301-9627

Table of Contents

To have a page for my book recognition and the help they gave. Wife for her with a manuscript, Debra Johnson. Davon Jackson for the help he gave in putting the manuscript in numerical order. And to my daughter Maya Johnson for the help she gave on my first book.

A Lie

The truth will rush against a lie.
Going forward with a lie.
Trying to tell the truth in vain.

Start with the truth and end with a lie.
The truth is hard to find.
You will not find a bright light.

At the end of a lie.
Because lies are told with dark intentions.
A lie tried to overcome time.

Time passes and the lie cannot hold up.
Time will bring the truth forward.
The lie told looks for the truth.

The truth shines with incredible brightness.
Through the darkness of a lie.
You can trace the consequences of a lie.

Your eyes open and you are the life of the lie.
No lie can rest on the surface of the truth.
To conceal a lie.

It is like trying to hold back the rain.
Only time will tell when the rain falls.
Wait for the truth to become victorious over a lie.

By
Rufus Johnson

A Normal Person

Normal people are the usual kind of people.
Most everyone is a normal person.
Normal people are not secluded people.

They are the type of people.
That will try and try again.
To keep from being a failure.

Their spiritual economy keeps them moving.
They move about and prosper spiritually.
Spiritually invested in Christ.

I caught the alarm in time.
Hands and hearts are forever filled.
With love for everyone.

Throw themself in Jesus's love.
Become a champion for His cause.
The truth is that God bless normal people and babies.

He blesses them because they tried so hard.
Time after time we wanted to give up.
Normal people move forward every day in life.

A normal person does not give up easily.

by
Rufus Johnson

Answered Prayers

When every one of our prayers seems to have failed us.
 It's not God's fault but ours.
We lack the ability to follow through on our prayers.

We do not have the insight.
To see the history of His works.
With His insight.

He discharges His answered prayers.
Through lapses of time.
That explains our slow progress in answered prayers.

Delayed prayers are not a failure.
Answered prayers are always on time.
Pray for victory in every area of your life.

Be available to pray.
Prayer channels His spirit to you.
Be fully convinced that your prayers will be answered.

Believe in His infinite love.
Do not despair but wait.
Know that one day a thousand years.

And a thousand years one day.
To answer prayers.

by
Rufus Johnson

Be Content

Vain and self-important person.
Thinking you are great with your own eyes.
And that you are great in God's eyes.

But you live in discontent.
Thinking that everyone has more than you.
Complaining about what others have.

This discontent will not stop.
Until you give up this discontented attitude.
Carry no feeling of grudge toward others.

All will carry a bad deed by you.
Live not in vain or discontentment.
Humble yourself to life.

If you call yourself a great person.
Then you should be capable of great deeds.
All your work you want for nothing.

Be content with what you have.
Then bless others with what they have.
In the end, the soul offers nothing.

But the work of your hands.
There is no gain without pain.

by
Rufus Johnson

Believe

It's your prerogative to believe.
To believe in good over evil,
peace over war
Love over hate and order over disorder.

Many feelings are connected.
In your belief.
The objectives are many.

Your objectives keep you on guard.
You are not ordered to believe.
You should believe in the wonderful.

Power that touches the heart.
It will throw light on your tomorrow.
A bright light that overcomes.

The dark objectives.
The time will come,
When you will reap your rewards.

You have sown the seeds of life.
Now you reap.
God is sowing His abundant love for you.

His blessing has come home to you.
You are not of affluence.
Patiently you waited.

For God's invaluable gifts.
Of mercy to be shown to you.
You consciously believe in Him.

by
Rufus Johnson

Blind Faith

Aim too high, you will make mistakes.
To keep from making mistakes.
You aim low.

Timid in your movements.
You are poorly advised.
All you can do is to turn the next corner.

You turn to faith for deliverance.
Resting on eternal truth.
That you are walking blind sighted.

Believing in the unseen God.
Faith is often blind.
Blind sighted in your faith

You are walking by sight not by faith.
Your deepest thinking.
You wonder if you are on the right track.

Under the guidance of the eternal light.
Your blind faith has sight.
Through your blind faith.

You hold on to full expectations of deliverance.

by
Rufus Johnson

Born Status

Just because a person was born lowly.
Low status position in life.
Your condition of living.

Determine your position in life.
You feel self-conscious and ashamed.
Of your born status in life.

Your disposition status.
Give you an attitude toward all.
This attitude you develop.

Does nothing for your status.
It will bring a native force into existence.
That will suppress your advancement of status.

Promote yourself by changing your attitude.
In the way you view life.
You can change your status in life.

By changing your attitude toward life.
Which gives you a greater purpose in life.
Despite your birth status.

by
Rufus Johnson

Carried Faith

Most of us are weak.
When it comes to understanding Jesus.
Our Lord, savior, and master, the King of glory.

Lord, it took courage to carry the cross.
We admire you even more.
Be faithful to your faith.

Believe and walk patiently.
Long years may pass before you realize.
That your faith can live a long time.

A tree that grows out of a rock.
Live a long time.
Your faith will carry you a long way in life.

Let your faith stand for you in this life.
Be confident in your faith.
Your age is measured in years.

How many prolonged years of energy you have left.
Your faith is a wonderful aid to longevity.
Carry your faith.

Like your faith carried you through this life.

by
Rufus Johnson

Careless

We have fallen into careless days.
We must step out into careless ways.
People are carelessly living with anger.

People mentally confused in life.
Many are discontented living carelessly.
Wandering about here and there.

Nothing to improve your case of careless living.
Get into pursuit of the essentials of life.
Respect the existence of others.

Life blood is precious to us.
To carelessly end another life is a serious thing.
To be stopped by a careless act of violence.

All hopes and dreams come to an end.
 Snap from the face of life.
The end came by a dreaded act.

Careless acts unloaded on someone.
Careless acts brought sorrow and suffering.
Careless ways have consequences.

by
Rufus Johnson

Character Assault

People do not like to be made fun of.
No one likes being made fun of.
In an unkind way.

Your intentions are to humiliate.
Whoever is at the end of your taunt.
You think that taunting.

Has no effect.
You are a negative influence.
On their character identification.

You are scornfully laughing at their character.
Your method of communicating is not working.
You are making a bad impression on your character.

Your reputation lacks integrity.
You never know how.
Your character assassination affects someone.

Some people are not strong enough.
They cannot take it.
Your assault on their character.

Danger you are walking on thin ice.

by
Rufus Johnson

Conflicts

All is slow to end a conflict.
Between family, friends, neighbor, and enemy.
 Year by year, your conflict continues.

A way to a destructive path.
In pursuit of increased confusion.
Supported by destructive behavior.

Opinions of bitterness.
Bring hate to you.
Cries of the innocent.

Between two enemies.
Pour words of love to a conflict.
Move on by every means.

To love and peace for one another.
Look for ways to end a conflict for the right reason.
A collision of love needs to occur.

To end the conflict.
It's not vain to look for peace in a conflict.

by
Rufus Johnson

Control Sins

Self-restraint, you cannot control.
The effect of your lack of control.
Acts in the realm of sin.

Stand your ground from sin.
Married between sinning and not sinning.
Your relationship with God is in danger.

Entangle connection with no gain spiritually.
Not a good picture to draw back on.
Poor visions of the past.

History shows past sins.
You have been deceived.
Many pleasures seem harmless.

Rooted itself to your heart.
You have a friendship with sin.
Sin is the enemy of your life.

Sin like weeds they keep regrowing.
Like weeds hard to control.
Waiting for the right opportunity to come back.

Sin penetrates the spirit over time.
And take your virtue away. Repent.

by
Rufus Johnson

Days Gone By

The days of God move like the wheels of time.
You need encouragement.
Do not be afraid of days to come.

Be brave and stand ground.
He will accelerate the wheels of time when needed.
Gazing at the days gone by.

Coils lay around tomorrow's dreams.
The coils of tomorrow are cloudy hazes.
That turns to rain showers.

Rain waters the days with encouragement.
The encouragement counts.
Like raindrops on each day.

Each day your encouragement grows in faith.
For the coming tomorrow, hold on a little longer.
You've been living through days of pain, nights of suffering.

Now you are walking in glory, the pain.
You lived through the troubles and the suffering.
That brought you victory.

The bright days of tomorrow will be well worth living.

by
Rufus Johnson

Diminish Truth

A friend said something, About you,
that's not true.
Their lying tongue is but for a moment.

Their lies unconfirm your friendship.
Their lies created trouble for you.
You feel swindled.

A bitter experience to lose.
Confidence in a friend.
A person you thought trustworthy.

Turn out to be a liar to your face.
Your trust in people diminished.
You say that you will not be.

Overconfidence in someone again.
You cannot live in this world.
Without trusting someone.

Everyone, not a liar.
You miss your friendship.
It all comes back to God.

He knew humanity long ago.
When He said to trust in no man.

by
Rufus Johnson

Disguise Faith

Society without laws is chaos.
Your belief without righteousness.
It is evaporative sentiment.

Prayer without duty may be.
A detachment of the wing from the bird.
Terror faints the heart.

Fame paralyzes the spirit.
Pluck up courage for self-defense.
Your faith is composed of layers.

Have faith enough to understand.
The difference between the right and the wrong.
Calculated devices meant deceive you.

Disguise faith meant throwing you off guard.
Disguise in any matter of faith stealing.
Disguises walking in plain sight.

And in broad daylight.
Remember faith without work is dead.
 Make use and exercise common sense.

by
Rufus Johnson

Divine Plan

We are subject to divine thoughts,
Elevating strengthening guidance.
You are deeper in your own nature.

God's nature is to be the Supreme Being.
The Supreme Being does all,
His one thinking. All creations are His.

He found his own way.
His divine thinking brings us to perplexity.
God's divine thinking is the instrument of our judgment.

God's divine thinking far surpasses our wisdom.
His divine plan is the birth of our faith.
His purpose will not be unfilled.

His divine wisdom has a means to all ends.
Following His words is the beginning of our wisdom.
His divine lessons triumph over all centuries.

Through centuries nothing has.
Prevail against God's divine plan.
One of God's divine plans is.

For us to live in peace together.
To stop killing one another.
If we do not stop.

It makes us one step closer to our end.

by
Rufus Johnson

Do Right

To live a righteous life.
Focus on the right thing to do.
To stand your moral ground.

Your conduct determines your virtues.
Be careful not to be self-virtuous.
Overconfident in your moral standards.

You hold claim to your morality.
Your moral principle stands alone.
Against the wrong being done every day.

The path to righteousness is narrow.
Stand firm on your path.
To do what is right.

You try to be steady and unwavering.
Yet yielding to compromises in every way.
Doing what should be done.

The natural order of things.
But doing what is wrong rules the day.

by
Rufus Johnson

Driven

Through the years you made.
Your way by working for a living.
You were not forced to work.

No one impels you or constrains you.
Vigorously each day.
You drove through the years.

Through all the financial setbacks.
Through all the employment setbacks.
You were driven to move forward.

There is a vital force.
In you that keeps you driven.
People made surprising drives against you.

Onslaught of confusion is unexpected.
You still pursued your mission.
No mission is without problems.

All your problems work their way out.
Your success, you feel already at hand.
Your triumph qualified you for success.

Through all, God has been your driven force.

by
Rufus Johnson

Each Day

The first appearance of light.
The day dawn the morning begins.
The sun rises over the horizon.

This begins the process.
Today that will decide tomorrow.
The day and night divides.

Each one has a fresh start.
Each one runs on their own beat.
The time of day.

Bring the end nearer and nearer.
The years coil around you.
You tremble with fear.

With more years to come.
These days are hard.

by
Rufus Johnson

Enemy Within

Spiritual warfare against an enemy.
That lies within and without.
Wrestling not against flesh and blood.

But against principalities and power.
Fighting the enemy within your own heart.
Having courage to fight the enemies of your heart.

They live to return another day.
Your sins play their role.
Facing evil by day and night.

It's a universal battle for your heart.
Your self-indulgent life does not help.
The fruits of faith need help from above.

A grander spirituality might be needed to save your soul.
Jesus the stronger spiritual might.
Leads us to the mighty King of glory.

The Lord saves with His salvation.
Blessed be the spirit of true life.

by
Rufus Johnson

Expectations

Expectations of your future depend on God.
It takes time for your expectations to come through.
Through the pain of years.

Working long hours to accomplish something.
The under- crying pain of years.
The heart filled with emotions.

The heart grieves over foolish memories.
Your expectation not to aim too high.
Just the general expectations in life.

You expect to live in freedom and happiness.
To see a vision with no complaint.
You have expectations of surviving your trails to come.

You are not drifting away.
Be well and keep His words.
Make another day.

To walk diligently in His walk.
To serve, to be in His counsel.
You expect to live right.

And walk through life.
Not accomplishing all your expectations.

by
Rufus Johnson

Failures

Your lack of success.
Do not make you a failure.
Something did not work like you expected.

Not because of insufficient effort on your part.
There is a valuable lesson in your failures.
You learn what not to do the next time.

Do not be overconfident, then fail.
Careless you went about with incomplete support.
You did not have sufficient resources.

Humiliating failure over and over again.
From lack of resources.
Like leaning on a leaning tree.

Not full of self-confidence.
You are concerned about your reckless actions.
One of the causes of your failures.

Do dilute your lessons of failures.
The voyage you made.
Have made you a stronger person.

All lessons are brought up front. For your cause.
In the end, you did profit from your failures.

by
Rufus Johnson

Firm Soul

Stand your ground against evil deeds.
Because the battle has begun.
The battle for your soul.

Hold firm to your soul.
Your soul is the closest.
You will get to heaven.

That is the spiritual part of you in this life.
No one left soulless.
Your soul prepares you for life to come.

Your whole life.
You are soul-searching yourself.
Looking for your true motive in life.

You must avoid dangerous principalities.
The powers of darkness of this world.
You wrestle not against your flesh and blood.

But against your evil deeds.
Do not let evil deeds exploit your soul.
You must hold firmly to your soul.

by
Rufus Johnson

First Glance

Look, what do you see?
Everything made from man.
Everything is made in some shape or form.

Except what you see.
Your eyes can lie to you.
At first glance, you cannot know.

If something is real or not.
You cannot know what the object is made of.
At first glance, how do people perceive you?

They gaze at you with wandering eyes.
They cannot see beneath your skin.
They do not know your case.

The fact is they have never met you before.
Our connection is only at face value.
At face value, you must be alert.

Pay attention to what is going on around yourself.
Be on guard and be watchful.

by
Rufus Johnson

Fraud

Acts of deceit discovered too late.
Trickery ground for false pretense.
A dishonest transaction has taken place.

Loopholes of lies, you've been deceived.
An impostor of a person has betrayed you.
Their acts of deceit are fraudulent.

They are on the opposite side of the truth.
Your personal interest will not carry the fraud.
Fraud brings nothing good to you.

Life is not worth living in fraud.
Your fraud has been miscalculated.
Your hope of benefit has been misled.

Their trickery is to cheat you out of money.
People work hard to earn money.
Their fraud will not pay.

What they gain, they lose.
Because if you cheat, you commit fraud.
You will get caught eventually.

In case you do not get caught.
Fraud will be your grave.

by
Rufus Johnson

Gifted

We are gifted with faculties.
That minister in some way.
For purpose of your being.

One faculty depends on the other.
The arms and fingers work together.
The leg and foot help one another.

To help us stand and walk.
The brain controls it all.
To work in coordination together.

Each one must be in continuous use.
To remain functionally useful.
We must use our limbs to keep them.

When you were young.
Your limbs grew in strength every day.
You move around without caring for the world.

You grew old, your faculties still working.
Your faculties, your talent.
That you depend on for work.

You are blessed to be born with your faculties.
But to keep them through adulthood.
Another blessing beyond thanksgiving.

by
Rufus Johnson

GOD AND YOU

I have God and you.
What more can I ask for?
Because God and you.

Made my dream come true.
We came together.
In the middle of the swing.

Holding on to the chains of love.
Swinging back and forth.
Holding on to God.

There is a constant in this love.
That is God and you.
God gave us this love.

God and us in harmony together.
Continually you bring God in the amid of us.
You act on God's behalf to bring love between us.

God and you raise my hope in life.
You lift me up to joy.
God and you are a true trace of beauty in my life.

by
Rufus Johnson

God Truths

Speak God's truth with all your heart.
The honest truths of life.
A good lesson for us all.

Let God's truth lead you.
Follow His truths through life.
Tell the truth at all costs.

Prolonged truth cannot be a hindrance.
Character report.
The truth persists over lies.

Your character triumphs through a lie.
God's truths cling to you.
You kept under pressure.

To tell the truth.
You are a servant of the truth.
Which you cannot resist.

Do not be afraid to speak the truth.
Fear can be a hindrance.
To tell the truth.

Speak your burning truth.
Apply God's truths to your life.

by
Rufus Johnson

God's Spiritual Kingdom

Evidence of a spiritual kingdom.
God is forever present in your mind.
Our life has two parts: spirituality and the world.

We are all in need of the guiding light.
The world and we are one.
Our existence in this world.

Everything depends on our will to survive.
We need the energy of faith to survive.
Our spiritual evolution proceeds.

Faith is a profound conviction.
Of wisdom and righteousness.
Confirmations of the mind.

A guide to claim righteousness.
And harmony with equal justice.
Evolution to survive.

Survival of the fittest.
Belonging to God's spiritual Kingdom.
Life has a divine end for each one of us.

by
Rufus Johnson

Grinding Work

Life will not spare you from grinding work.
To make a living for survival.
Days of laborious, fatiguing work.

To have to work a thousand days.
In weary steps.
You think your working conditions is poor.

There are others in worse condition.
Hard grinding every day from work.
That kind of grinding work.

That makes you a productive citizen.
That makes you an honest person.
When you were young.

You could do grinding work.
Years pass by with weeping eyes.
You look for comfort to relieve your soul.

From this grinding work.
Far from your end you prevailed.
You stayed with the grind.

Until you see better days.
You retired; your body could.
Not take any more grinding work.

by
Rufus Johnson

Harm Done

Accounts bearing on your life.
They are starting to add up.
Harm being done to others.

Without intending harm.
Ignorance and guilt at the same time.
A double condition of ignorance.

Not knowing what you are doing.
What you are doing involves guilt.
Your ignorance is a self-justifying plea.

Own up to your conduct.
To harm others in any circumstance is wrong.
Even if it's meant for good.

You cannot dismiss harm done.
Harm done is the wrong step.
An error that cannot resolve itself.

Bring your harm to forgiveness.
Trace your faults to selfishness.
Which is the real cause of your mistaken acts.

Wrong done can harm.

by
Rufus Johnson

Hearted Person

You have a giving heart.
Desire to see others happy.
Kindly and large hearted you are.

You enjoy and like giving.
You found pleasure giving.
You like to make others happy from your giving.

You do not wish to multiply your riches.
But your riches will be multiplied by giving.
You love the freedom of giving.

Your generosity is nothing but a drop.
What is needed in the ocean of giving.
Nothing but a faint shadow of giving.

You still want to give more when possible.
It is better to give than to receive.
It pleases God for us to give.

He shows His infinite love by giving.
Nothing will be withheld from you.
The windows of heaven will open for you.

You will receive your higher blessing.

by
Rufus Johnson

Higher Call (1)

No one can do a real service for the world.
Unless he or she is a fearer of God.
He or she loves their God.

And righteousness more than self.
Serve the Eternal before all else.
Leaders are not chosen spiritually.

We look for the cleverness of character.
The power of wealth.
That catches all eyes.

That will not raise our insight into morality.
Liberty of mind is what's needed.
We all must be ready for our higher call.

That is to treat our neighbor.
Like you want to be treated.
We are worldly in nature.

Our best guide is spiritual.
Each one of us must be thoughtful of God's ways.
We have a duty to pursue peace on earth.

Redeem yourself from selfishness.
And to live the life of your true
self.

by
Rufus Johnson

Higher Call (2)

No one can do a real service for the world.
Unless he or she is a fearer of God.
He or she loves God.

And righteousness more than self.
Serve the Eternal before all else.
Leaders are not chosen spiritually.

We look for clever characters.
The power of wealth.
That catches the eye.

Will not raise our insight on morality.
Liberty of mind is what is needed.
We all must be ready for our higher call.

That is to treat our neighbor.
Like you want to be treated.
Some people are mean in nature.

Our best guide is spiritual.
Each one of us must be thoughtful of God's ways.
We have a duty to pursue peace on earth.

Redeem from selfishness.
And live your true self.

by
Rufus Johnson

His Grace

God's tendency is to view our hearts.
Our hearts represent who we really are.
He uses our hearts to deliver His grace to us.

His spirit operates in us.
He knows the hurt our hearts have been through.
He knows our human nature.

No one can recall God's first.
Work of grace in their life.
He has a connection within our lives.

His grace is part of our salvation.
We give ourselves up for His salvation.
We are blessed by His grace.

Fall on our face for His grace.
Ask what we must do, to keep His grace? At
times it feels like His grace over us.

A manifestation of favor.
Set for your salvation.
Your heart will not be cleansed.

Without His grace.
A piece of heaven rests in your heart.
By His grace.

by
Rufus Johnson

Husband and Wife

Husband and wife brought together in matrimony.
A union that should never part.
Striving together moving forward.

The man falls short for her.
She helps to prevent his success.
By second-guessing him.

Undermining will not raise him.
That will keep him down.
You are at the altar of failure.

A combination of man and woman.
Man and woman strength will work together.
She makes his interest her own.

To achieve social status and wealth together.
To raise him and rise with him.
She makes the opportunity at home.

She can fix the opportunity at home.
And fix her smile to the end.
A happy wife makes a happy life.

by
Rufus Johnson

I Am Race

We are of the I Am Race.
Because we are born in the image of God.
He is the Great I Am.

He is Him that we wish we could be.
We of the I am race.
Look to God with love.

Your love has in case us.
He modulates His love for us.
Through His spirit.

This love that God has for us.
We must want it.
God is warm, tender, and passionate.

His love for us never stops.
His desire for us not to war.
Is met with deaf ears.

We have a love affair with hate.
The benevolent love of God.
Must prevail for us to survive.

This occupation we embrace with hate.
Is not of God.

by
Rufus Johnson

If It Can, Sir

If it can-sir will attack your immune system.
If it can-sir will give invasive growth.
If it can-sir will put you in an abnormal condition.

If it can-sir will take over the whole body.
If it can-sir will attack the blood.
It will attack the blood cell.

If it can-sir not your friend.
If it can-sir will attack the brain.
If it can-sir will attack the skin.

If it can-sir your enemy in hope.
Our medical research has come a long way.
To fight back against if it can-sir.

We have pharmaceuticals and chemotherapy.
Do not let if it can-sir, take over you mentally.
By giving hope, a chance for a better tomorrow.

The doctors have done their duty.
Nature will proceed to heal you.
You must get some courage for your healing process.

When you are faced with overwhelming circumstances.
There is nothing, no help but God.

by
Rufus Johnson

In Motion

The moon and sun are important to us.
The moon encourages us with light at night.
The sun gives light and energy by day.

If the moon and sun stood still.
Will produce injurious consequences.
The end which can hardly be conceived.

If the rotation of the earth.
On its axis, it suddenly stopped.
All life, all loose objects will fly forward.

With violent force.
The mighty divine power of God.
Can control all motion.

He can adjust to all forces of nature.
He leaves them to operate by themselves.
In a uniform way.

Without disturbance or interference.
That's God's way of giving free will.
All life remains in motion.

All things kept in motion.

by
Rufus Johnson

Life Values

Money drives all of us.
We do a lot of different things with money.
Money draws all kinds of contempt.

Money is the root of drugs and most evil.
Money is the reason to steal with skill.
The lack of money leads to poverty.

Money puts food on the table.
Money is not going to come to you.
Without putting in work.

We work hard for that money.
Not putting money over all values.
Make a living without money.

It's hard to value life without money.
When you are sick.
What is your life value?

Any amount of money to keep you alive.
Everything is going up except for life expectancy.
No matter how much money you have.

You cannot take anything with you.
When you pass on after this life.

by
Rufus Johnson

Little Words

Words the way we communicate.
The way we express meaning with one another.
To what has been said or done.

Our words form our language.
We speak with different accents.
That is hard to understand.

Yet words link us together.
In our words.
We can talk about our differences.

Our differences are blocked by harsh words.
Actions overshadow our words.
No words can make up.

For what has been done.
Words mean little.
When action is in need.

Sensible talk must prevail.
To settle our differences.
So little words must make a difference.

by
Rufus Jonson

Live Humbly

Fall to your humidity.
With the attitude to preserve your dignity.
Live with humidity by acknowledging you wrong.

Living with your humility.
The beginning of you being lifted up.
To throw light on your bitter heart.

It is a noble virtue to live with humility.
To forgive family and friends.
For their wrongdoing.

Your humility does not make you a footstool.
The word says that we.
Should seek first the Kingdom of Heaven.

And his righteousness.
Then all things will be added to you.
You need vigilance and prayer.

To live humbly and with humility.
Accepting humility is a decision on your part.
To overcome evil and not let it affect you.

God has not signed you out.
Your heart thrills over the peace you feel.
From your humility that you share over others.

Be humble at heart, keep living humbly.
God got you.
Your humble ways have paid off.

by
Rufus Johnson

Living in Fear

You are afraid of today's times.
A feeling of anxiety everywhere.
It's not an illusion that society.

Beating hearts shake to the nerve.
Sleepless nights apprehend you.
Your emotions are out of control.

Through the dreaded emotions.
Panic starts to set in on your condition.
ou are living with your circumstances.

You are living with fear.
A lot of misery comes from fear.
Our source of distress is fear of guns.

Fear that far too many guns.
Are in the wrong hands.
Fear of being shot.

Fear of being sick, fear of being homeless.
To save yourself from fear is a difficult task.
Renew your strength against fear.

Encourage yourself faithfully.
Life assured anxiety, no cause to fear.
A great word of confidence says.

Fear not, says the Lord.

by
Rufus Johnson

Loyal to God

Bent on your loyalty to God.
You made up your mind to believe.
He is the first and the last.

Look and see what He has done.
He's entitled to your loyalty.
You have chosen what's best.

You chose to be His servant.
You have set down and reason with yourself.
Feeling with weighed options.

Making God your supreme over all.
You see the advantages of serving Him.
Satisfaction of entering peace.

The kind of peace that brings you peace.
To your heart, mind, and soul.
You are living in peace.

A clear choice with your mind made up.
You sing at the peaceful sunset.

by
Rufus Johnson

Lust

Lust is a disease that destroys.
Your moral character.
Havoc will be induced by continuous use.

Sexual play has its consequences.
Your over-desired sexual appetite.
Considered lust.

Lust always has its prey to go after.
The eyes lust before the mind or body.
They lust after what you see.

Take control of your lustful ways.
By over mastering your sexual desires.
Control your lustful appetite.

Lust will bring you to the brink of failure.
Lust will make you do unusual things.
Going unchecked will be dangerous for your health.

Lust the parent of sexual exploitation.
It will bring out your personality.
Lust a cunning device that robs life.

by
Rufus Johnson

Lying Character

Living with a character of being deceitful.
You are driven to deceive.
Weeds flourish in bad soil.

The truth is hard to find in a body of lies.
Bound by your decision.
You commit to your lies.

No gain will come to you.
Your lying lips will bring you no delight.
For some lying lips a life characteristic.

You perform with artful deception.
Your character cannot be concealed.
You told too many lies.

You are not worthy of the truth.
Grace will not be found in a body of lies.
The lies will go through your soul.

The truth will not be found in your mouth.

by
Rufus Johnson

Mischief

The wrong spirit brings mischief.
It breeds rivalry and enmity.
It will lead to disastrous consequences.

Make you turn away from family.
You are on a mental error of being misled.
It is a bad spirit creeping on you.

The results are scary.
It becomes the rivalry of your life.
Like husband against wife.

Father against son, sister against sister.
Brother against brother.
Nothing good comes from mischief.

It only creates animosity.
Strong hostility toward one another.
Plant a seed of comfort.

Become the source of a good spirit.
Have a vigilant eye to see mischief.
And the forbearance to spot trouble before it starts.

Priceless blessing to see trouble before it starts.
You see divine love through all the mischiefs.

by
Rufus Johnson

Misdirection

You move in different directions.
At all times having no place to go.
You are wondering, no, not that way.

All directions seem good to you.
Your way not in all directions.
Get disappointed by making the wrong turn.

Your wisdom is not always at its best.
For the most part.
You don't know any reason why.

You're misdirected where the fault lay?
You search in all directions.
For someone to blame.

For your misdirection's.
You are looking for all types of explanations.
While the real problem is close to home.

by
Rufus Johnson

MOM'S FOREVER

Forever a moment away.
Forever an hour, who can say?
A mother's name is called forever and a day.

Who can see tomorrow?
Forever, many years away.
Forever only time can say.

Mom and forever never part.
From beginning to end.
Mom's love always lives in the heart.

Live life cautiously.
For Mom says, forever is only a moment away.

by
Rufus Johnson

Natural Sense

You lose blood from broken skin.
You are bleeding.
Blood flows out of your open wound.

You must get closure.
Antibiotics, alcohol, etc.
To keep the wound from infection.

That will trouble the whole body.
You seek medical help.
For your wound from suffering.

Only by your natural sense.
That you know to get help.
For your wound of suffering.

Search your heart of senses.
To know your thoughts and feelings.
If there is any weakness in you seek help.

Have the sense to be led to the everlasting.
Healing power of Jesus Christ.
Through the father God.

by
Rufus Johnson

Next Generation

Years added up to a generation.
A new generation slips into our existence.
It's our duty and responsibility.

To look after the children of the next generation.
It does not take long.
For a generation to come and go.

Realizing that our journey has an end.
How life has been.
Looking for an infinite future.

When time has passed.
A new generation had come and gone.
Try not to have too many neglected years.

Because of our short time.
Our days have been numbered.
That we can apply our heart to.

Our wisdom can act on our behalf.
Be a guiding light.
For the children of the future.

by
Rufus Johnson

Normal Blessings

God's normal blessings are everyday blessings.
We were blessed to have woken up this morning.
We are blessed with the ability to speak.

We are blessed with the ability to see.
We can walk on our own.
We can feel the warm water.

These blessings are of no perspective.
These blessings are for everyone.
These blessings are normal blessings.

Every day we work our blessings.
To the best of our ability.
Do not take advantage of God's normal blessings.

By using power over those less fortunate.
There are those born less of God's normal blessings.
God has a special blessing for them.

They are the same as you and me.
Remember God has no perspective person.
What is normal?

Can be taken away.
From us at the blink of our eyes.

by
Rufus Johnson

Not Worldly

Courage, righteousness, and talent.
Shows the making of a good person.
Personality makes itself visible.

Personal effort, not selfish in ego.
Higher self of a good person.
Not worldly.

Proceed with the opportunities to be successful.
You inherit a brain and a soul.
You practice self-suppression.

Through this perplexing world.
Everyone needs to live with a purpose.
You do profit from being rich.

Living in amusement and luxury, to be well-known.
If God and Jesus do not command, you.
You will certainly lose all that makes life joyful.

Living life to show.
Enthusiasm, strength, and eternal joy.

by
Rufus Johnson

Opinion

Everyone has an opinion.
We have different opinions.
Having a position not to surrender to other's opinion.

You stand by your opinion.
Ordinary matters, your opinion counts.
Someone thinks their opinion is better than yours.

That should not matter, it's just their opinion.
Many people have agreed with you.
On a lot of different matters.

You are not alone in your opinions.
You express personal judgement on subjects.
You work for someone; they form an opinion of you.

Their opinion of you affects your job.
Your positive certainty gives your opinion merit.
Everyone's opinion counts on something.

Everyone's opinion has some value.
We live in this world together.
We must respect one another's opinion.

We differ in matters of opinion.

by
Rufus Johnson

Our Churches

Our churches are our place of worship.
One day worship per week.
Your obligations are not meant to be mechanical.

God Himself must enter your heart and mind.
He lives in the church and in you.
A merging of hearts is what is needed.

You are His church, each one of you.
To live right in the full sight of the Lord.
You are His structural worship temple.

Our church should unite and save us; they do not.
You are at a point in time.
Where you need to come to God.

The full light of heaven needs to fill your air.
The air you breathe needs to expel evil.
God has a great desire.

For you to have peace in your heart.
You need to open your mind.
To the great gates of righteousness.

To fill your heart.
You are His audience of His praise.

by
Rufus Johnson

Our Differences

Boys, girls, men, and women.
Ladies and gentlemen, he and she.
His, hers, guys, and gals.

All describe the same.
Two genders with different words.
We both have differences.

Some are physical, some are mental.
We act differently.
We have different ways of doing things.

We speak and talk differently.
We wear different types of clothes.
We comb our hair differently.

We wear different types of shoes.
Our shoe sizes are different.
Women wear a bra.

Men do not.
Men and women reproduce together.
One cannot make three without the other.

by
Rufus Johnson

Our Problems

God tracks problems in our community.
Then he tracks the problems of the family.
And finally, your problems.

We all bear our own problems.
The foolish see and not grieve.
Over what we see happening to the world.

The fact that we all have problems.
All problems are going on at the same time.
And no one person or we as a people.

Can do anything to solve our problems.
We are individuals when it comes.
Your own problems of the world.

No one can take your place.
You are the one person in the crowd.
That can make a difference.

Set before His sight.
All problems are open and set right.

by
Rufus Johnson

Passing On

A lot of people are always contemplating.
Who passed on the day before.
More concern about the passing-on.

Then the living.
Looking at the death notice every day.
The spread of their coma, to family and friends.

Their deeds of innocence lead to death.
Their act of caring for the dead.
Leads to death.

Their harsh vision of reality.
Caring for the dead, leads to your death.
Jesus said to care for the living.

The dead will take care of themselves.

by
Rufus Johnson

Past Years

God's plan of discipline for me.
It is to put me through the test of time.
My discipline has paved the way for my old age.

I do not like to think that I am getting old.
The youthful years, playful years, are over.
My pleasures in life seem to have faded.

My life passed by so quickly.
Before I knew it, years passed by.
My youthful years were gone.

Full of youthful years gone by.
My years of strength have reached their limit.
I still feel healthy and active.

But my age says that I am getting older.
Telling me about life in years past.
That is where my discipline pays off.

Did I live my life for good and for God?
I do have regretful feelings of years gone past.
And my life accounts for me.

Through the years gone past.

by
Rufus Johnson

Pleasures of Life

God has created.
The right, the wrong, and the spiritual.
The three in opposition to one another.

The right and wrong are like a seesaw.
When everyone goes up, the other comes down.
There can be a right and wrong force that is spiritual.

God makes things of this world to be enjoyed.
Provided we use them and not abuse them.
God does not condemn the pleasure of life.

It is when the pleasure you seek.
Are preferred over your higher calling.
Your pleasures led you down the wrong path.

Life is a struggle between the pleasures of life.
You struggle to control your pleasures.
Do not let your pleasures control you.

When you enjoy a large share of comfort in life.
You become selfish.
That's proof how pleasures perverts God's gift.

And turn His gift to your pleasure.

by
Rufus Johnson

Plants and Animals

A plant knows where to grow.
There is always a place for a plant.
And a plant for a place.

The animals have their place too.
They spread all over the world.
Live in the wild.

The elephants roam and live off the land.
The beaver lives by the streams.
The birds fly.

The great order of fish swims in the seas.
All places are desirable and undesirable.
They live and thrive in the wild.

They take cover from danger.
Their natural survival instinct kicks in.
Their survival is the goal.

Plants and animals are gifts from God.
Each one has their purpose.
They help us to survive.

Our world would not be the same.
Without plants and animals.
They are our source of food.

by
Rufus Johnson

Poor Blessing

Greed and selfishness control the day.
That's the order of the day.
The rich get richer and want more.

People are getting high all around.
High on alcohol and drugs.
The murder of the soul and body together.

Repent for the soul.
Ease off for the body.
Accumulated injustice makes life worse.

Luxurious living mocks the struggling poor.
They hand down crumbs and clothes to the poor.
The poor are thankful for all the crumbs and clothes.

Handed down to them.
The poor in need of a constant supply of blessings.
The poor conquer the rich.

By following God's words.
And living a Christ-filled life.

by
Rufus Johnson

Relying on God

God rewards your faith.
He gives you victory in the end.
Jesus satisfies the longing soul.

Your spirit will not be broken.
Lift your eyes to the Lord.
Your future will not be without hard work.

Without anxiety and danger.
He gave you the gift of survival.
For you to do things for yourself.

His purpose is for you to depend on Him.
The great thing for you to do is.
To keep up a connection with God.

It is of importance that you do.
To have your heart firmly established in Him.
Get into the habit of relying on God.

Read His words.
That is the basis of your faith.
Train your mind to His words.

Search the word for your spiritual growth.
That's your plea of confidence.
That will help you grow.

by
Rufus Johnson

Respecting You

I try to be humble.
In admitting my faults.
I made many mistakes.

Not being too proud.
To say that I have regrets.
I am sorry.

That my mistakes have affected you.
I respectfully would like to lift you up.
I will not reduce you below myself.

We have a common pain together.
Our conditions are similar.
You are worthy of my respect.

You will not suffer humiliation from me.
I will not be deceptive to you.
I am not an impostor to you.

I am not pretending to be your friend.
I just care for and respect you.

by
Rufus Johnson

Revenge

You feel retribution.
Which demands urgency on your part.
Restless spirits see no circumstances.

Seeing nothing, knowing nothing.
It's not your duty to seek revenge.
The desire for revenge can be strong.

A feeling that will not go away.
It starts to live inside of you.
Talking comes to no solution.

Witness its operation and eye for an eye.
Taking a life in action.
Allowed to stand, you become the victim.

Part of you becomes rage.
The spirit of revenge is blind.
Hurtful practice trying to hurt others.

Practice that will not stimulate the soul.
A personal feeling you must overcome.
The law of love is not in action.

Revenge left in your hands.
Not the way of the great avenger.
Vengeance is mine said by the Lord.

by
Rufus Johnson

SAVE

Everything and everyone need saving.
We need to save our money.
We need to save our jobs from AI.

The water system.
Need to be saved from contamination.
The air needs to be saved from pollution.

The animals need to be saved from extinction.
Society needs to be saved from corruption.
The government needs to be saved by itself.

We have civil rights.
We must fight to save them.
We need to save our sanity.

You need to save your social status.
Everybody needs saving.
We are in a terrible position.

We are in trouble everywhere.
We need to be saved.
We need to save our souls.

Save, save your soul.

by
Rufus Johnson

SEARCH

All intelligence comes from one intelligence source.
All earth properties have existed since eternity.
Say the world was not created.

Science today has been snatching.
Thunder and lightning from the sky.
We have put our fingers on everything natural.

All that appears natural comes from man, so it seems.
All natural forces have been touched by science.
All happens in a natural way we say.

We have searched for the Heavens.
And found over a billion other galaxies.
God has been very busy.

Every opinion has been submitted.
We search the universe.
And cannot solve our deepest problems on earth.

We search, looking for a trace of God.
He cannot be found.
Unless He wants to be found.

by
Rufus Johnson

Self-Worth

Respect that OK, if you do not.
A feeling of not getting your worth.
You feel good about yourself.

There is a lot of disrespect going around.
You cannot combat all.
The disrespect headed your way.

So, you deal with life situations diligently.
You cannot lose respect for yourself.
Keep that respect lifelong.

Admiration for self-worth.
You have the right to self-worth.
Self-worth cannot be overstated.

Consider yourself a quality person.
Your attribute qualifies.
You to be a quality person.

You can identify with your self-worth.

by
Rufus Johnson

Serious Purpose

Nothing is insignificant.
In the Bible.
Nothing can be disregarded the least.

The written word stood the test of time.
His words spread and have value.
The spiritual message of God.

It has a serious purpose.
To save the wandering souls of the believers.
Trying to master the difficulties of life.

Settle faith in God.
God's inspiration is vital.
To the broken disheartened.

There is a sure way.
When your faith has won over.
You are not a poor victim any longer.

Because you are a seeker of God.
With God, everything is serious.
And with God, there's always a way.

by
Rufus Johnson

Serve God

We tend to compromise.
To serve God half-hearted.
If you serve Him at all.

You serve Him completely.
The decision must be made by you.
Your heart must serve.

Consistent with the word.
His words will bring some rest within you.
You can meditate on His words.

Nothing inserted in the Bible.
Is without a purpose.
His words are meant for edification.

A way to live through this life.
He knows our future before it happens.
He knows our trials and problems.

Will be continuous.
Generation after generation has the same problems.
He knows that we need His help and guidance.

We do have a mutual benefit.
To read His words and believe in Jesus.

by
Rufus Johnson

Showing Through

You hardly ever meet people.
That you are better off after meeting them.
Sometimes people are in disguise.

Their smiles are not real.
You look for bright and modest people.
People that are cheerful at heart.

Honesty will speak through their words.
Decisions are made from words.
Not sure of your decision with confidence.

Look again at their attitude.
See their conviction.
If they are a follower of the faith.

It will show through their words.
Hear the words of the faithful.
How we cry and try to be understood.

Sometimes the disguise we see are smiles.
Trying to hold back the tears.
It is not a disguise of character.

It's just the pain showing through in smiles.

by
Rufus Johnson

Stand

You cannot live in someone else's space.
Their impression of mind.
Not the same as yours.

You cannot walk.
In someone else's footprints.
Your feet do not fit their path.

You cannot grow in someone else's mind.
You can only grow in your own mind.
In which you stand.

Today you stand in your own footsteps.
As you stand so shall.
Your strength increases.

No doubt that the more you stand.
The more convinced you become.
That your strength comes from God.

Look at the sky where you stand.
You have gained a lot.
Standing by God.

Patience is very valuable.
When you stand by God.
The hour awaits.

When small and great.
Will stand before God.

by
Rufus Johnson

Stay Gray

Your hair is so beautiful.
Filaments growing on your scalp.
All mammals have some form of hair.

We live with hair on our head.
For your hair to remain beautiful.
You must take care of your hair follicles.

All your life, treat your hair like a newborn baby.
To nurture your hair sometime.
Keep it cut, wash, and condition.

To apply some oil for the follicles.
You and your hair have reached maturity.
Where some gray has set in on your scalp.

Your hair has reached the glory years.
So relax and let the gray stay.
You have aged gracefully.

And you look respectfully.
Show your gray with gratitude and thankfulness.

by
Rufus Johnson

Steppingstones

The storms of the past are overlooked errors.
You have a gleam of right light shining on you.
You are a helper of eternal grace.

You must show a higher range of passion and effort.
For the right against the might.
Or liberty against oppression.

You might not get far right away.
You work, your righteousness for good.
Now your faith is working for you.

The word is true for the faithful.
The words of energy and prosperity are good.
Stay true to the best service of the heart.

For the soul suffering has growth.
Your past storms are but steppingstones.
For your soul's future.

All those steppingstones are meant for your benefit.
And to throw you back to God's purpose.
You thrive despite all those steppingstones.

by
Rufus Johnson

Stop Abuse

Lord lay up for me.
A crown of righteousness.
On earth and in heaven.

Let me not trust in my own work.
I seek your salvation first.
Then I stand and fight.

Just to be able to complete the course.
I will keep the faith.
To overthrow every strong hold of abuse.

Reduce abuse by law and order.
It will take all of us to stop abuse.
There is a lot of work to be done.

The day ends with no work done.
You are the instrument to stop child abuse.
Play by God's rules.

The work starts with you.
Your work needs to be close to God.
Precious in the sight of the Lord.

Is not to participate in any type of abuse.
This is a start to your crown of righteousness.

by
Rufus Johnson

Stored Treasures

You have plans of extreme riches.
Penny, wise and foolish wishes.
You reap where you sow.

Securing wealth looks for a productive investment.
All that glitters is not gold.
Layup not for yourself treasures on earth.

Where moths and rust will destroy.
Life and money are unstable like water.
A fact to be noticed.

A fact not to be forgotten.
Your money will get old.
Your car will rust.

Your house will decay.
No matter how cunning your plans are.
You cannot take any of your possessions with you.

What you build up on earth, you lose.
What you sow to the flesh, you reap nothing.
Live to be comfortable for today and tomorrow.

Receive what God gave you today.
When you are gone.
Be glad to leave it all behind.

Because your treasures are stored up in heaven.

by
Rufus Johnson

Teachers

A teacher instructs our children.
They get knowledge from the teacher.
A child depends on knowledge from the teacher.

When the children are confused.
The teacher guides them through.
Teachers do not know everything.

Through years of being taught.
We become self-reliant.
Then you go on your own.

Very fast you are not a child any longer.
You must give up childish things.
You learn to be on your own.

A habit of leaning on others.
Keeps us children.
You work through difficulties.

Life is a training school.
When you become an adult.
You will always be learning.

by
Rufus Johnson

That Day

Your deeds no doubt have spoken to you.
The best part of you has moved on.
When passing on after this life.

Your light went before you.
Your darkest day.
Your faith passes on with you.

The day of your great event.
You do not know who is beside your site.
The glow of your spirit.

It has influenced the world.
You are a witness to your life.
Testified before God that day.

Those who live after.
Will not be you.
The clouds took over that day.

It was a new day of fresh morning faith.

by
Rufus Johnson

The Few

We are left on this earth to survive.
God designed to place us here.
A place where we can exist.

Provide us with shelter and a place to live.
 The property in the hands of the few.
The few have accumulated properties.

The ideal economy is for everyone.
To have a decent place to lay their head.
The few have increased their land possession.

Desperate to see true land ownership.
The fruits of the land are absolutely in despair.
Hopelessly getting justice for the poor.

You never own property.
Because if you do not pay your taxes.
Your property falls into the hands of the few.

When you are up against the world.
Ask God to take interest in your comfort.
To give you no poverty or riches.

To keep you fed and be good to me.

by
Rufus Johnson

The One

The mighty power of God.
His words have mighty power.
He created all in all with His command.

He is the promise keeper.
His promises have all been kept.
His promises move through centuries unfailing.

God has attributes.
One of His attributes is.
That His word cannot be made void.

God has character.
He shows us righteousness and mercy.
God is the one who sees all and knows all.

God is the one who picks prophets.
God is the one who gives.
Prophet's visions of the future.

God, you are the Father to us all.
He is the Father, the Son, and the Holy Ghost.
God, you are the one we pray to.

God, you are the reason for our faith.
Without God, we have nothing.
Believing in that is good.

Keep faith alive in the One.

by
Rufus Johnson

The Same

No one person can duplicate another.
The four people are different.
We all have different temperaments.

We are of the same community.
We are of the same family.
We have different attitudes.

We have different personalities.
We live in different homes.
Some rent, some own their homes.

Some have no place to call home.
Everyone needs a place to call home.
What it means to have a home.

Is to put a roof over your head.
That becomes a greater part of your life.
You pay your rent or mortgage every month.

To ensure your place to stay.
You have a sense of responsibility.
You show interest in your own welfare.

We are all different and share the same responsibilities.
That makes us the same.
Just in different bodies and homes.

by
Rufus Johnson

The Struggle

Parents and children must separate.
When children become of age.
If they stay, they cannot grow.

Life has no time for playing around.
The struggle is real.
Your struggles have touched your heart.

And reach for your soul.
Embrace your past struggles.
They prepare us for trails of the future.

It takes courage to stay in the struggle.
Your courage gives you persistence.
To overcome your struggles.

Because you have some money.
You have not overcome the struggle.
Money does not make you immune to struggle.

You must struggle to keep your money.
Each family member has a part to play.
Each person represents themselves.

In the struggle.
Expect great things to happen to you.
Prepare for great things to come.

by
Rufus Johnson

The World

This world that we are born into.
We will have troubles.
We will have trials and tribulations.

Our outcome every day is uncertain.
God says that we are born of sin.
We are born into complicated circumstances.

From the start, we must be nurtured.
By our parents and their parents.
No one is left alone; we all need help.

The help that we need is lifelong.
Lifelong trials and tribulations.
It seems that we are faced with doom and gloom.

But there is light at the end of the world.
And that light is Jesus Christ.
Our Father which is in Heaven.

And there be His throne.

by
Rufus Johnson

Unwanted Experiences

The very thing you put from your life.
Come right back into your life.
With flowing tears and pain.

Seems to manifest itself.
A feeling of unwanted past experiences.
I gathered heated emotions.

Unwanted visions of the past.
Fearing entering unwanted days.
Fear takes control.

Your conscience touches.
Having reason to fear the past.
Troubled years have passed.

Mingle years with the future days.
We live for today.
Unwanted experience not making.

The same mistake repeatedly.
We should learn from our experiences.
Looking for something better.

I have an urgency of putting.
Your unwanted experiences in the past.

by
Rufus Johnson

With God

No deeds of doing right.
Wick deeds of disgrace.
I need to talk about deeds of disgrace.

A hollow pathway to reach hell.
Depressed feeling of hopelessness.
Increased depression flows like water.

It runs down to the bones.
Discouraging no attempts to be saved.
True acts of not seeking God.

Rejoice not in your sins.
You are on the wrong side.
Not knowing God.

Like the earth without the sun.
Your body without a soul.
A person will follow anything.

A person without a clear path.
Has no clear conscience.
A person with God has a way to save their soul.

A person with God has direction.
A person with God.
A great benefit to the world.

Gifted with a higher form of life.

by
Rufus Johnson

Woman Rights

Females are not inferior to male.
Evidence shows that she has an internal instinct.
She likes mothering, nurturing, and directing.

They are not to be subjected.
To man with no rights.
A woman presents her claim to be equal.

She is important to the world.
A lot of decisions are not made in her favor.
Women exert influence over other women.

She should enjoy the respect due her.
Women are productive in society.
They are individual members of our community.

They form the organization of our families.
Cultivate her to grow into womanhood.
She is equal to man in all rights.

by
Rufus Johnson

Working

Looking to get rich without working.
No labor or trouble on your part.
Idle time cannot be your objective.

Your objective in life loss.
Sitting around with idle time.
Cannot be the best part of you.

Self-indulgent of idle time.
It is a waste of time.
This will not make you rich.

You must turn your hands for your desires.
Working is a blessing.
You benefit from working.

Your labor keeps you healthy.
You find your strength builds every day from working.
Your labor gives you honor.

It guards you from stealing.
Promote a healthy mind and body.
Increase your energy in life.

Your spirit will rest at night.
You are a heavenly worker of all things good.

by
Rufus Johnson

Working for a Living

The economy of working for a living.
You have the right to work for a living.
You are not asking for more than your share.

By working, you are multiplying your income every day.
If you are not working.
Then you should be looking for work.

Let there be no wasted days.
If you have means.
Then you should be working.

Nothing will be handed to you.
Do not look for your blessing.
Without diligently working for your blessing.

You must put in the work every day.
You have a need for productive days.
Go after that work, step to that work.

God's blessing is obtainable.
His blessing does appear.
When you are in need.

by
Rufus Johnson

Worldly Wealth

All have come to you, in the wrong way.
You aspire to go even higher.
You soar to fall.

All hope rests on your wealth.
Intensified blindness of money.
A greedy eye cannot see.

Beyond making money.
The error of our vision.
To only see money and wealth.

Our impression leaves a stain.
Ingenerated hearts crave for more.
Displease with the way you get your money.

Convicted of being on the wrong path.
Reflections on irreversible events.
You think about the things.

You do for your money to be dismissed.
All your riches lead to nothing.
What is the end of a selfish and greedy life?

by
Rufus Johnson

Wrong Path

Few people are drawn to a person of high character.
So many follow the path of a bad person.
The young look up to crooks.

The criminals lead the way.
The criminals rise above your level.
Their crimes are a burden on society.

You are tormented by your narrow path.
In the valley of crime.
The bottom is swelling with criminals.

The criminals have made their choice.
Their decision is in crisis.
Their morals are too far off to see.

The criminals will not pass you bye.
They will not hesitate to pull you in.
Get into your consciousness.'

They will not be happy.
Until they bring you down.
Say to them as for me and my house.

We will serve the Lord Jesus.
And I will find nobility in my character.

by
Rufus Johnson

YES

Yes, to you Lord God.
Yes, to your Holy Spirit.
Yes, to you Jesus Christ. Yes, to the Son of God.

Yes, to the rise of the Son on the third day.
I say yes, Lord, from the bottom to the top.
I say, yes, Lord.

In the morning when I wake up.
In the evening when I was asleep.
I say, yes, Lord.

When all my confusion set in.
I look to you for your guidance.
By saying, yes, Lord, to your will.

When I become weak.
I gather your strength to stand.
To break through the pain of my weakness.

I say, yes, Lord.
Through all the difficulties in my life.
I say, yes, Lord, to you.

For a clearer understanding to be safe and secure in life.

by
Rufus Johnson

You Are

You say that you are free.
Then work your freedom to stay free.
By doing what is right and staying out of jail.

Your heart will not be oppressed.
You are not to misuse your freedom.
You have been free for so long.

You forget why you are free.
You are free because others work for their freedom.
For you to stay free.

You are the fruit of freedom.
You are at liberty to grow in faith.
You are into justice and truth.

You are completely free to believe in God.
Life advancement appears accessible now.
You pass the struggle of being fruitless.

Pass the agony of your craving soul.
You are standing firm to your end.
Looking past, all danger.

And looking for clarity that justifies liberty.
That is worthy of the majesty of eternal justice.

by
Rufus Johnson

You Fight

We are born with a special gift to fight.
Some are born incapable of fighting.
Performing regular activities can be difficult.

You can fight over rumors.
You search for this rumor and cannot find it.
There is no one to fight.

A boxing contest, testing your ability to fight.
You fight for civil rights.
You fight because you are being accused of something wrong.

Your country fights and goes to war.
You fight because you are angry with disagreement.
The law fights against crime and people who break the law.

We fight child abusers.
We fight against the flu and other diseases.
Maybe you must fight.

This disease is called cancer.
 Now you must fight to live.
You are engaged in combat for survival.

Revise your heart and claim God.
Claim the very heart of you.
A claim that makes you a fighter.

by
Rufus Johnson

Your Faith

Your faith started like a mustard seed.
Your faith extends beyond things seen.
Your faith is your expression of hope in humanity.

Like a mustard seed, your faith grew in confidence.
Like the spread of God to the world.
Your faith cannot be true without deeds.

Your deeds should be greater than your faith.
You are not barren by your deeds.
You are walking by your work and faith.

You yearn for your deeds to be accepted.
By your outpouring of affection toward humanity.
Your cup overflows with hope and joy for humanity.

You wander with gratitude in your faith.
Your faith keeps you from going astray.
Keeps you on the correct path.

You make a conscious effort in your treatment of others.
Your deeds are starting to add up.
Now you have proven your faith.

The faithless will be confused with no faith.
Be a living faith and a professed believer.

by
Rufus Johnson

Your Heart

Your heart in contempt.
Toward the faithless, they forget God.
Do not let their poor ambition of God.

Get in the way of God's divine plans for you.
Do not let jealousy linger in your heart.
It's a tact to have a thorough understanding.

Of your heart.
Highest glory is to be one with God.
His will is forever your will.

When you speak, everyone knows it's God's will.
His will be done in you and on earth.
Rehearse this fortified plea every day.

State and speak it from your heart.
A breath of truth will melt your heart.
So speak the truth from your heart.

You cannot hide the truth from God.
Know that this is true.
Let the truth be stamped in your heart.

The truth will be told anyway.
By your heart.

by
Rufus Johnson

Your Name

We are only here.
In a matter of time, a short time.
Your name is entitled to be remembered.

For something good for all times.
Your service is only one state to please God.
Over the years you are still in people's memory.

Started by your earlier work.
You advocated for other rights.
A spiritual calling of duty.

Faithfully you discharge the call.
 The calling radiates through time.
Your name will be to serve with love.

Blessed by your work.
You establish your claim.
That you are entitled to be remembered.

By your name.
Your name here for a set amount of time.
Your name is all you have.

You destroy that, you destroy everything.

by
Rufus Johnson

Your Peace

Attempts made against your peace.
Their hearts set against your peace.
They will not let you keep your peace.

Peace will not be kept by violence.
Violence beats peace.
Peace gives in to violence.

Peace grows weak by violence.
Your peace cannot rest with violence.
Your peace will be brief.

Wishing peace will stay in your life.
You want peace to fill your eyes with blessing.
Place peace around your life.

Caress your peace and look for joy.
Peace be with you.
Let not violences disturb your peace.

Try to walk away to keep your peace.
You can stand and fight for peace.
 After all the fighting is done.

Can you live with your peace?

by
Rufus Johnson

Your Place

A place that has a special meaning.
Meaning of a place with words.
The occurrence took place.

Give it the name.
A place for you is to restore hope.
To get away from the poverty and misery of others.

A vineyard in the valley of hope.
This place has a door.
That shut out troubles.

Your defeated troubles block with hope.
This door blocks lost happiness.
The truth is that God is at the door.

Becomes your blessing from hinderance.
Everything has been arranged in your place.
Your troubles block everywhere.

Everything works for the goodness of God.
Even the sweat for your place.

by
Rufus Johnson

Your Salvation

Meanness breeds greedy treacherous contempt.
You stood against all treacherous contempt's.
Where others have failed.

The hour has come for your salvation.
Thank God for your moments of grace.
God has brought you victory despite it all.

Your compassion is not discontent.
Your weeping cries are heard.
The welfare of your life was protected.

Through your faith, you can save others.
Your acts of good will reach others.
God justifying merit of grace.

Be a living faith for all things.
The doors of salvation will open wide for you.
Your salvation will affect others.

You have obtained a new life through Christ.
You will be a tree planted on good, watered soil.
Let not your heart depart from God.

Your salvation comes from God.
Your salvation belongs to God.

by
Rufus Johnson

Your Transgressions

Your transgressions are real.
The cause of all your troubles.
You are living against God's moral code.

Your behavior is beyond the limit.
Your conduct needs guidance.
You violate the order of living right.

Having to step across the line to do wrong.
Everything in your life.
Will be affected directly or indirectly.

By your actions of doing wrong.
Your life of peace will be shaken.
Your transgressions will flood your life.

You have transgressed against your own soul.
You are trying to doom yourself.
The lesson learned from your conduct of actions.

Trouble following you.
For what you have done.
It will affect your entire existence.

Your transgressions will not rest.
Until they find their way back to you.

by
Rufus Johnson

www.ingramcontent.com/pod-product-compliance
Lightning Source LLC
Chambersburg PA
CBHW020623130626
46552CB00003B/1079